MESSAGE SONG

DELIVERING IMPORTANT AND POWERFUL MESSAGES THROUGH LYRICS AND MUSIC

Author: Mosi Dorbayani
SOCAN/ASCAP

Publisher: WAALM Publications, UK & Canada

Library & Archive Canada
ISBN: 978-0-9940842-5-5

Cover design: Christelle Walker
Inside images: WAALM Archive, Public Domain & Creative Commons

This book marks the author's publication of 50th original song.

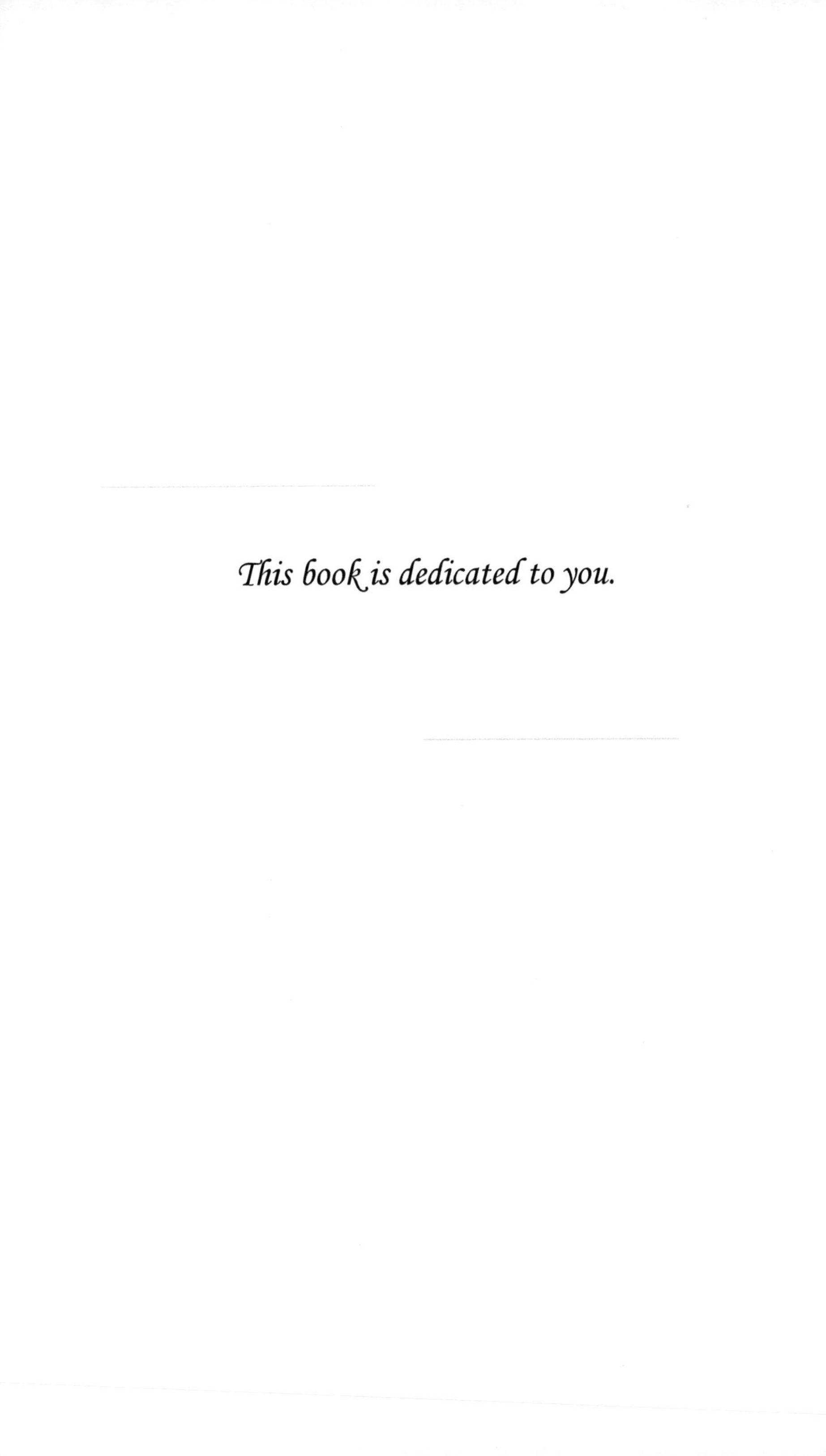

This book is dedicated to you.

CONTENTS

FOREWORD

"There's nothing either good or bad, but thinking makes it so," Shakespeare's Hamlet

Words are thinking tools. They can be used to shape thoughts.

Language is our major form of communication. How we use it shapes our identities. We understand, learn and pass on our social and familial roles and responsibilities through the language we use. Such communication can be influenced for the purpose of good through meaningful songs.

Since songs can potentially reach deep to all aspects of human being, i.e. physical, emotional, intellectual, and spiritual, it is perhaps one of the most effective means of education and form of expression, where the music is not just listened to, but felt and understood.

Through exploration of lyrical words, songs become a practical medium to engage listeners in a meaningful conversation on social and humanity issues.

Because songs can evoke deep personal meanings, socially aware and responsible songwriters often use 'message songs' to remind listeners of human integrity and social values. Usually through such songs, they invite listeners to think, evaluate, contribute and get involved in important matters or those of historic moments.

Since 'message songs' can best describe and reflect the social in the individual and the individual in the social, it is naturally the most engaging type of song to establish 'dialogue', 'understanding' and 'unity'.

A well-written 'message song' has soft penetrating powers. It can prevent the use of hard power, and can encourage tackling crisis through 'Cultural Diplomacy'.

Perhaps we all studied and/or remember the role of 'Jazz' during the cold war and how it could bring people and continents closer to each other.

'Jazz Diplomacy' as it was known then (1950s -70s), proved to be the most powerful tool of the American culture to diminish Communism beyond *the Eastern Bloc.*

"Cultural Diplomacy was persuasive during the cold war because its "Ambassadors" i.e. performers, writers and thinkers were perceived to be independent of the government." Cynthia P. Schneid, Brown Journal of World Affairs.

Singers and songwriters are among the best who can play the role of a diplomat or an ambassador in their societies. The messages they can deliver, however informal in context, are highly effective in raising awareness. Today, we can see many celebrities like 'Bono', 'Geri Halliwell' and 'Shakira' who have become determined advocates to end the world's poverty, injustice and inequality.

But of course one does not need to be a world celebrity artist in order to be influential. One can still influence their society and community for betterment in small steps, simply by not being ignorant and taking active roles.

"...Silence encourages the tormentor, never the tormented." Elie Wiesel, Writer

Songwriters or lyricists in particular – are often dubbed as 'wordsmith'. They are the ones who can craft words to push the ignorance away and facilitate awareness instead. They are the ones who can provide the proper "thinking tools" to the masses.

When they intelligently and memorably write their heartfelt expressions, the public will inevitably gravitate to such material, which makes them to get in touch with their emotions and value their shared vision.

Whether you consider yourself a songwriter, song poet, lyricist or librettist, you are on a stellar path through which you can make a real difference. ***Your job is more than just finding the right word which fits, it is to inspire 'hope and courage' to face challenges of constantly changing environment.***

Mosi Dorbayani

SENSE AND SENSIBILITY

Writing message songs is a highly sensitive and delicate matter. If not well-thought, it might directly influence the audience or fans' reactions or cause disappointment and create unwanted media frenzy.

Before we go any further, note that when we say delivering 'important' and 'powerful' messages through music and lyrics, we are not considering a personal message of an artist to their ex-lover as the result of their break up or divorce.

Here we are trying to look at it in a wider but deeper spectrum and over the subjects that can be genuinely called "a cause".

To begin with, let us answer the following questions in turn:

1. What is ‘important’?
2. What is ‘powerful’?
3. How to ‘write’ a powerful message song?
4. How to ‘deliver’ it?

WHAT IS IMPORTANT?

This is simply true that perhaps what is “important” to me or close to my heart, may not be necessarily ‘important’ to you or close to your heart. Therefore, the key here is to identify:

A) As important as it seems to me, is this equally important to my targeted audience?
B) If this subject matter is close to my heart, and I see it necessary to address it through my song, how can I make it much closer to my audience’s heart, so that it can have a significant impact?

To identify the above, I suggest songwriters to carefully study several aspects of their cause:

- What is the shared vision?
- Which angle of the subject matter makes more common sense?
- What can I say about it differently?
- Is there any aspect of this subject matter that had not been touched before?

Most probably, once you identified the above, you would find the answer to whether your cause is just as ‘important’ for others or not. This mini study will assist you and perhaps your sponsor / executive producer to save time and money before you get yourself engaged with the production of a message song.

WHAT IS POWERFUL?

Now the element of 'Powerful'. Let us briefly touch the word 'Power'. Well, defining power in terms of Mechanics and Electronics is pretty straight forward. We learned at school that it is the rate of doing work or equivalent to an amount of energy consumed per unit time.

In terms of Social and Political Sciences, it is the ability to influence or control the behavior of people.

It is often associated with 'authority' legitimate by the social structure.

But in musical terms and musical literature, the word 'power' begs for different measures and definition. In mechanical and social applications and norms, eventually power ends. But in reality, the true 'Power' never breaks, dies nor ends.

In fact, in the context of music and musical literature, we are ALL looking for this truly 'everlasting power' to apply in our music. That is, making a music, powerful enough that hopefully never dies.

When we call a song "powerful", it usually means it has an impactful influence.

But if in a short time, the influence fades away, then the power of the song is close to the one defined in social science, i.e. it had the ability to influence and even affect the behavior of the listeners but it was eventually short lived. Here, the key is how to write a powerful message song that not only lasts longer, but also remains relatable for all times – generation after generation.

Here, one may argue that if a message song is to serve a particular cause or event, then it is natural for that song to short-live and fade away almost immediately after it serves its purpose.

Well, if your message song is for example a 'Protest' song, that might be the case. Once the protest is over, the song naturally gets cold. However, if your message song addresses relatable and wider global issue and could be associated with both local experiences and global affairs at the same time, those type of songs most probably will not get easily outdated and when the time comes, they would be remembered and reused over and over again.

We all know that history repeats itself until humans learn their lessons, right? So, why not writing a message song that not only addresses the current issue, but also may well be used when similar issues occurred again. When jotting down a song, at the very least, you should have that *"time factor"* in mind.

There are tens of meaningful message songs that were written in the late 19th and throughout the 20th centuries, which are still relevant today and are referred to by people, communities, producers and media.

What was their secret? Well perhaps the secret is in:

- Finding a worthy cause, both close to home and abroad to scale in a timely manner;
- Posing the right objective questions, including those suggested by your cause and answering them all in honesty;
- Deciding whether to write 'literally' or 'figuratively' – whether to use a direct approach in conveying your message literally or 'metaphorically' or even 'proverbially';
- Placing the key words in the right places in your song's structure.

HOW TO WRITE A POWERFUL MESSAGE SONG?

In writing a message song, you need to make all your efforts to create a piece that not only has something new to say, but also stands the test of time with maximum long lasting impact. In order to secure a successful and impactful project, there are five guidelines for you to consider:

1 – Differentiate 'Modern' from 'Classic'**.** In my view, what passes the test of time, is relevant and still exists, is called classic. What is new and is yet to pass the test of time, is called modern.

You are recommended to apply every creative element at your disposal that has more chance to stay around for a longer period of time.

And in this respect, never ignore the past and do not shy away from learning the lessons from the history.

Consult with the classic message songs that are still relevant today and with the ones that are contemporary.

Try to learn about their *mission, vision and values*. Find out why they were made the way they were created and what elements contributed to their successful impact.

2 – Since here the core is the message itself, clearly, the primary emphasis should be given to the lyrics/words. However it is always possible to add lyrics to a pre-composed music, in my experience, it is better to let the music and melody get its impression from the words. For writing message songs, *I recommend you start with writing the lyrics first.*

3 – In your writing, *always consider the influence of the words on your listeners*. One might ask, 'but how on earth can one predict human reactions to the words?' Well, here psychology comes handy. The best predictor of future human behavior is their past behavior.

And since listeners by essence and definition are all human; therefore, it is possible to study this. You need to conduct a bit of research on what sort of words and phrases positively influenced people in the past.

Try to form a small focus group and read out your lyrics to them; ask them to tell you about their impressions; question them about their take from the entire lyrics; ask a participant to read out your lyrics while you watch others' facial, body language and emotional reactions.

Make sure your words and verses are indeed transferring what you meant and intended.

Moreover, do your best to make sure your words are not just an echo or stereotype. ***Avoid proving a point with your lyrics. Keep it polite, sensitive, tactful and humble.***

4 – Match your melody, style, tempo, and music arrangement to suit the message you are trying to convey. Make sure listeners find it easy to follow your words.

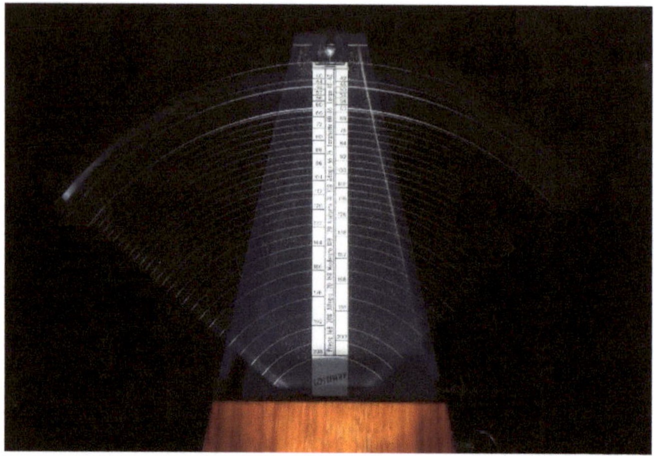

It should not be too fast for listeners to find it difficult to comprehend or too slow to easily get bored.

Once again, you can use a focus group to examine their impressions and reactional behavior on your song.

5 – If you are not the singer of your message song project, it is absolutely vital to have it recorded by someone who can hook with your lyrics and melody. Your vocalist must be a total match. Do not underestimate vocal qualities, timber, vocal range, vibrato etc. It is recommended that you consider a few vocalists and run a test to see which one could deliver your project best.

Now in the following page, I will share with you a few structural writing tips and strategy.

STRATEGY FOR WRITING A MESSAGE SONG

Unless you are producing instrumental music, the lyrics are the most important part of your song. And among all types of songs (art songs, pop songs, folk songs, work songs, etc.) message songs require the highest level of attention and time on wording the lyrics.

However still simple in wording and grammar, message songs are considered intellectual pieces of writing or musical literature.

Writing lyrics to communicate an important message is not an easy task. In general, writing lyrics can be the most frustrating and difficult aspect of the songwriting process, especially for new songwriters who lack experience, and this could be even more challenging for authors who wish to write powerful message songs.

Typically, a song can be created by having an idea, a title or a hook, then building it up by asking questions about the title, then by putting your initial writing into segments and musical structure – playing it about with rhythm and fitting words around melody...etc.

In writing message songs however, I suggest a different approach.

I suggest NOT selecting a title first! Because, by selecting a title first, your message may get derailed and instead of staying objective to your core message, your words may shape your lyrics to simply satisfy the title or even your hook. Here are some strategic tips for you to consider:

1 – Answering 'whys' behind objective(s): First and for most, identify the 'whys' behind your objective. *This is to assure yourself if you are up to the task and if you have enough reason and conviction to see it through.*

For example, there is a cause which found its way to your heart, or you witnessed an event or faced an issue in the society and now you want to write about it. So, to begin with, you should at least answer five whys in writing (not in your head):

- Why does this matter to me?
- Why should I be the one who is writing it?
- Why should my writing make any difference?
- Why NOW, why not before or later?
- Why should the audience care what I have to say?

Your honest answers to your 'whys' behind your objective should provide you with a solid self-realization and determination to either take up the task of writing a message song or simply leave it.

If you are convinced that you have all the reasons and the means to do it, then you need to move on to step two, i.e. conducting a short study or research and writing your 'Advocacy and Espousal' brief.

2 – Writing 'advocacy and espousal' brief: Before the actual lyrics writing begins, you are recommended to carry out some basic studies and research on the topic, casuse, event or issue for which you want to write a message song.

Due to the sensitive nature of writing message songs, you are advised to write yourself an 'advocacy and espousal brief' –and treat it as your presentation for a proposal.

Writing such briefing will help you to have a deeper insight and understanding about the subject matter; it will assist you to identify the key issues related to the topic and will help you to select the right words and tune for your message song. It also indicates if indeed you have something to say – albeit, a suggestion, call for action or some form of solution (if and when applicable).

However writing a detailed 'advocacy and espousal' may not be required for every type of message song, depending on your subject matter and its level of sensitivity, you are recommended not to overlook its importance.

An 'advocacy and espousal brief' normally consists of:

- **An introduction to subject matter;**
- **A brief about the cause or event, issue or problem;**
- **A noteworthy angle or aspect to the subject matter;**
- **The posing suggestion, solution(s) or call for action.**

Remember: *"Complaining about a problem without posing a solution is called whining"* Teddy Roosevelt

So, at very least, writing a research-based advocacy and espousal brief will keep you in check and prevent you from turning your message song into a whining, complaining or nagging one. Since your advocacy and espousal writing comes from some degree of studies, it facilitates you to address the issue through your song 'logically' and not just emotionally.

While you write such briefing for your own use, you should think of it as a "presentation" for selling an idea to a group of audience. Once your song is released, your research and briefing can serve you well during promos, talk shows, interviews, appearances, fundraising or raising awareness events. You may use your 'advocacy and espousal' paper to establish yourself as an educated songwriter with some authority on the subject matter.

An introduction to subject matter

In this part of your 'advocacy and espousal paper', you draft an introduction to your presentation. Think of it as an opening to a discussion, or a preliminary hearing. This is where and when you set your tune, draw your audience's attention with some intriguing info, words, phrases, questions or statements.

A brief about the cause or event, issue or problem

This is where you write your actual experience, finding, investigation, study or research on the subject matter. Think of it as presenting facts with supporting evidence or documents. This is where and when you want your audience to place themselves into that presented situation and you want them to relate to the subject matter.

A noteworthy angle or aspect

This part of your 'advocacy and espousal' assures the audience that you are not repeating the same old story. This is where you explicitly state there is indeed an unseen angle or untouched aspect to the subject matter that is worth looking at, and that it requires attention. Think of this part of your presentation as pre-proposal.

This part of your presentation should make your audience to think to themselves: 'what could be the solution?', 'how could this be addressed?', 'what shall I do to help?', 'what is my role in this?', 'how can I make a difference?' etc.

Presenting a noteworthy angle/aspect is the most important part of your strategy for writing a message song, i.e. making your audience or people to 'THINK'. And exactly right there when they are thinking, it is the best time for you to present the next and final part of your advocacy and espousal

The posing suggestion or solution(s)

This is the other most important part of your strategy for writing a message song. In this part of your presentation, you assure the audience that you are not just talking about the cause, event, issues or problems and that in fact you did your due diligence and are coming forward with some sort of suggestion and/or solution as well. This is when you propose a suggestion or solution to the subject matter.

Here, as a case study, I want to share with you one of my message songs, which I wrote based on the same principle or strategy by first answering the 'whys', followed by drafting an 'advocacy and espousal' brief or presentation before composing the actual lyrics.

If you are wondering, yes, the result was phenomenal. It was recorded by artists from 25 countries, spanning 5 continents in 12 genres – even recorded in other languages and well-received by many organizations around the world who shared the same cause or mission.

The background story to the case:

On October 10, 2012, Amanda Todd, a 15-year-old Canadian girl, committed suicide at her home in Port Coquitlam, British Columbia, Canada. Prior to her death, Amanda had posted a video on YouTube in which she used a series of flash cards to tell her experience of being blackmailed into exposing her breasts via webcam, and of being bullied and physically assaulted. I was saddened by this news, and however bullying itself was nothing new, the fact that it caused a 15-year-old to commit suicide shook me, hence I felt I should write a song on bullying.

What next?

Well, fact of the matter was that there were plenty of meaningful and touching 'anti-bullying' songs out there – some were even created just after Amanda departed. *Do I need to write one? Is this really necessary?* I asked myself. There and then, I decided to use my "coaching" skills and question myself by answering the five 'whys' behind the objective(s), followed by drafting a presentation as my 'advocacy and espousal' for my message song project.

Here is my abbreviated writings. I started by asking myself:

Why does this matter to me?

Well, like very many people, I personally experienced some form of bullying in the past. To some extent, I can feel and relate to this issue of bullying. However I do not have a daughter, but as an educator I am aware of this problem at schools and know that it could exist even at homes or workplaces. It matters to me because I am a member of the same society and it would be a shame not to play any role in at least raising some awareness about it.

Why should 'I' be the one who is writing it?

Because I am also an educator, and familiar with psychology of communication. I am a humanitarian and a Human Rights advocate. I have the necessary skillset including song writing to address this issue.

Perhaps as a goodwill ambassador for Human rights it is expected from me to do this. <u>I expect it from me</u>, and most probably people will accept it, if it comes from someone with my background. <u>And above all, this would be a responsible thing to do as a songwriter</u>.

Why should my writing make any difference?

Because my writing shall address this issue from a different angle and point of view. Because it shall address this issue like never before, and in a scale that influences society at large.

Why now, why not before or later?

Well, honestly, I was never moved by such a tragedy as the result of bullying before. And now I have the capacity, means, experience, and resources to create something impactful. I am committed to do it now rather than later, because the issue is on its highest peak and it is being discussed at every level. Later may become never!

Why should the audience care what I have to say?

Because my message song will not be another typical 'anti-bullying' song. It shall not only address the subject matter from a different dimension, but also invite listeners to pay attention to suggestions I am going to make. And because my message song shall not just comfort listeners, but 'coach' victims, and their relatives or public on how to tackle it.

What then?

My answers to questions above furnished me with a crystal-clear vision, mission and direction. Now I have the full intention and determination to do my homework and prepare my 'advocacy and espousal' presentation before writing the actual lyrics.

Based on my written commitment in answering the five 'whys', as well as my studies on the issue, I drafted my presentation as follows (Abbreviated from the 2012 studies):

An introduction to subject matter:

Bullying comes in different forms including 'emotional', 'verbal', 'physical' and 'cyber' and it is so sad to see our beautiful children, youths or even adults suffer from such behavioral assert and domination.

Why our country's most important future assets and brightest minds should become the victim of such abuses to the extent that they would rather take their own lives?! We must bring education and awareness at every level because we all know it well that bullying is no longer limited to the playgrounds, schools, or even workplaces.

A brief about the cause or event, issue or problem:

- According to statistics from CDC: 4400 young people commit suicide per year and 50% of that figure, i.e. 2200 suicides were because of bullying.
  - For every 1 suicide, there is at least 100 attempted suicide by children and youths.
  - 160,000 students stay at home and don't go to school every day because of bullying! That is over 3,000,000 student a month.
- In England, at least 20 Children and adolescence commit suicide a year because of bullying.
  - 69% of children reported bullying per year. More than 168,370 students stay at home and don't go to schools every day. That is about 31,000,000 school days lost a year.
- In Canada, 47% of Canadian parents report having a child victim of bullying.
  - 40% of Canadian workers experience bullying on a weekly basis.
  - 233 people between ages 10-19 commit suicide a year because of bullying.

Image shared under a Creative Commons License by Thomas Ricker
https://www.flickr.com/photos/trixer/3531445744

- In France, 17% of children in the study had been hit, 18% had suffered sexual harassment (being undressed, forced kissing or touching).
    - 16% had been given a demeaning nickname.
    - One in four said they had been insulted, with 7% saying they had been subject to racial abuse.

*References:

- Research by Yale University https://news.yale.edu
- Centers for Disease Control and Prevention - CDC https://www.cdc.gov
- Bullying Statistics: http://www.bullyingstatistics.

A noteworthy angle or aspect:

Psychological and social studies show:

1. 'Lack of confidence', 'courage', and especially 'absence of communication or talking to a mentor/close family member' are among reasons for victims of bullying having extended depression.
2. Often young victims of bullying feel their looks, appearance, size, or disabilities are among reasons for being badly treated by other.

Problem with previous song writing contributions:

Following my mini research on this matter, it came into my attention that however many of the previous spoken words and songs were nicely written, in most cases:

A. They often missed the points 1 and 2 above.

B. They are written and produced to often condemn the bully and their heinous act, but with limited attention or reference to victims' needs.

C. They usually state the obvious, portray or report a bullying incident or sympathise with the victims by yet again condemning the act of bullying.

D. The past productions often used ‘Anti-bullying’ terminology in describing their song title (e.g. X/Y: An anti-bullying song). Probably due to having that “anti” tune and mentality during productions, their contents are often found cliché. Perhaps it is time to change that tune, change our perspective and think differently before writing a new song to address bullying.

The posing suggestion or solution(s):

Typically, such songs target the bully and their behavioral assert and domination. Why not instead of targeting the bully, we target the victims as our audience and address the victims with a heartfelt message song?

I suggest writing a message song to the victims (not the bullies) through which we emphasize on their certain values, their importance, and coach them with a few words on the best possible course of action and dissuade them from doing regrettable acts under the external force of domination, which may result in loved ones’ devastation and despair.

And what next?

Well, as you can see above, my advocacy & espousal study and written presentation provided me with a framework and almost all I needed to outline what I wanted to include in my message song:

My message song outline:

- **Type of song:** A message song for '<u>humanity</u>'.
- **Target audience:** '<u>Victims</u>' of bullying.
- **Age group:** Mid-teens to young adults.
- **Type of message:** Both 'encouraging' & 'dissuading'.
- **Style of message:** Coaching or mentoring with a loving or caring tune.
- **The core theme:** Motivating victims to overcome behavioral assert and domination with courage, talks, and by embracing their uniqueness. And, dissuading them from doing regrettable acts that may cause despair for their family and friends.
- **Key words:** 'courage', 'strength', 'patience', 'positivity, 'uniqueness', 'loneliness', 'talk' and 'love'.
- **Main message:** Be a 'victor', NOT a 'victim'
- **Subtle message:** To face the issue with courage, instead of walking away from it (a poke to those who miss school due to bullying or those who are running from it to take refuge in solitary).
- **Acknowledgment:** Explicitly mentioning 'teasing', 'mocking' and 'bullying' as issues.

After figuring out my subtle message, main message, theme and key words – I was ready to select a title and a hook and insert my key words into the song/lyrics. So thereby, ***'Walk in Style'*** – A message song to victims of bullying was born and it became one of the world's biggest musical projects for humanity in its kind.

The project could create dialogue among people on social sites; artists shared their versions with their fans all over the internet; it drew the attention of media; educators and life coaches who shared the same vision used it to raise awareness; and of course, it reached to Amanda's mother, who on Facebook expressed her appreciation to all artists involved.

This could not be achieved without administrative support of *'WAALM Productions, UK & Canada'*. And hereby I would like to acknowledge the musical contributions of: 'Loghman Adhami', 'Michael Brass'; 'Terrance Rose'; 'JasWho'; 'Andysh'; 'Silent Company & E. Popp'; 'IXIISIS'; 'Serge – Neoclubber'; and 'Radhika Shankar' and thank all the vocal artists, arrangers, and sound engineers around the world, who selflessly shared their talents with me to realize this project for humanity.

In **Aug. 2017**, *'Walk in Style – the legacy'*, in RnB style was produced by the author & voiced by talented, Mike DeCole – as part of an EP album titled: 'May and Everything After'. This version got nominated for best lyrics at 8th Hollywood Music in Media Awards of 2017. For streaming go to Spotify or artist and author's music pages.

My precious darling please wear your smile

With courage you can conquer and walk in style

Be a victor, not a victim

Hear your heart, be yourself and stay strong

Though they may tease you, mock you, and bully you around

Should know that you're unique and for sure one of a kind

With patience let your soul be your guide in hardships

Don't hold back, talk, for sure you are not alone in this

Open your eyes and see those who love you

Don't leave them broken-hearted all in despair

Don't do something that we all deeply regret

Oh, be positive, a victor and not a victim

Hear your heart, be yourself and just stay strong

My precious darling please wear your smile

With courage you can conquer and walk in style.

HOW TO DELIVER A MESSAGE SONG

It is not just about 'delivering a message'. One can get the message from prose. It is about motivation, excitement and nostalgia that listeners can get from the entire production of a song. It is the emotional connectivity and the vibes that make it a different yet powerful form of delivery.

People can simply read a poem and receive any form of message from it, but it is the lyrical music – the chanting vibe of a song and melody that draw the major attention, attraction and raise awareness among people at large.

To that end, there are elements such as 'vocal', 'musical', 'visual' and 'time' delivery to consider.

Vocal delivery: There are times that a message song is best to be recorded with someone' voice that could do justice to the project. If your cause or message is important to you and to your society, then it is best to have it recorded by someone who shares the same vision and values, and who can perform it better.

If you are not a vocalist or your voice is not a good match, then it is important who voices your message song.

Based on your 'cause', 'context', 'type of message', and 'target audience', you need to decide what type of voice and which gender could best deliver your message. As the result of your focus group studies, you may even go for a duet or a trio if necessary.

Remember that some recording artists have lyrical and metrical vocal qualities and some have monotonous vocals. Some have skillful vibrato techniques and some have no ability to do vibrato at all. Selecting the right type of voice for your project is of highest importance.

Musical delivery: While message songs are often possible to be delivered in almost all genres, certain messages are best to be delivered in a particular genre or style.

For example, if your message has a sense of constructive criticism, perhaps Rock or Hip-Hop could serve you best. Or if your message is to encourage empathy, humanity, peace or dialogue, perhaps Soft Rock, R&B, Soul, or Crossover may carry those messages best.

As a songwriter, *you need to be prepared and willing to adjust styles to get your message across, if and when necessary*.

Album Cover for the song: Ocean without Shore

Visual delivery: Before people listen to your music, your image might be their only impression. Like any other type of song, the image you present for your message song must be appealing, intriguing and it should project the essence of your production. Your production must have the *"total package"* factor.

This also applies to your music videos. Your visual medium should complement and reinforce your message and not the vocal artist. For message song videos, the focus should be on the core message.

Time delivery: Message songs are time sensitive, so make sure that your release date meets the best timing for greater impact.

You need to apply a proper project management for your message song. Even if your message song is for a non-profit, charity, or a particular event with no commercial purpose, still you need to make sure it will bring you full success in terms of time and impact.

Remember, having fun and enjoying what you do is important, but it should be complemented with professionalism. *The more serious you take your project, the more powerful, long-lasting and impactful it becomes.*

THE COURAGE FACTOR

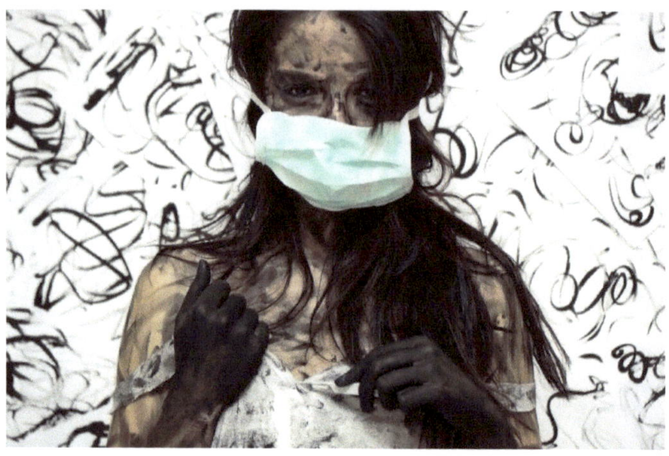

Whilst ideally every song should have a story to say or a proper message to convey, there are times that message songs may not say what is "politically correct" or "what is popular", especially if your message song is a 'protest song'. In such situations, **the courage factor is decisive**.

You need to have the courage to write and say what is 'right', and deliver it as you truly 'mean it'.

You must be courageous enough to stand by your words, and your words ought to be from your genuine belief and conviction for the cause close to your heart. ***Delivering message songs is a great responsibility. Your voice may become the voice of those voiceless, and your words, the words of those inarticulate.***

TYPES OF MESSAGE SONG

It is a powerful thing when a song finds its way to address the biggest issues in our social lives.

Yet sadly, even the greatest spoken words can stumble when you start to play it safe or bend your objectives to accommodate political favouritism.

Similar to political poetry, if a message song is a 'political song', it often has a tendency to become a lyrical news editorial, or a diplomatic essay song.

To avoid such pitfall, first and foremost you need to be fully resolved and determined to write what is 'Right' – far from favouritism, political affiliations, or fear from facing oppositions or criticism.

So far, I do not have any explicit political or protest song in my repertoire, and frankly, I do not feel comfortable to go into much details discussing protest songs without having enough hands-on experience. However, my studies suggest, perhaps addressing ***'policies'*** instead of 'politics'; ***'raising awareness'*** instead of 'giving warnings'; being ***'objective'*** instead of being 'subjective or personal'; stating ***'softly'*** instead of 'harshly' and making ***'suggestions'*** or asking ***'questions'*** instead of 'demands' could be a more effective way to address a political issue through songs.

Showing sensitivity in choosing your point of view matters immensely.

Why the choice of point of view matters? Well, here are some examples. However due to copyright and reprint licensing I cannot mention lyrics of the following songs to analytically compare them for you, I entrust by only mentioning their titles you would do some research, take a listen and study them for yourself:

Vietnam War Memorial - Photo via Flickr user Kalacaw under Creative Commons

During the Vietnam War (Nov 1, 1955 – Apr 30, 1975) many singer-songwriters lent their voices and talents to raise their concern about war by releasing political or protest songs. Some became hits and even a few artists like 'Phil Ochs' could literally make a music career out of protest songs.

Looking back today, if I name protest songs such as: '*Master of War* by Bob Dylan'; '*Handsome Johnny* by Richie Havens'; '*I ain't marching anymore* by Phil Ochs' or '*I feel like I'm fixin' to die rag* by Country Joe and The Fish'; *'Find the Cost of Freedom'* by Crosby, Stills Nash & Young', most probably a few would remember them.

Some may say, it's a generational thing, but I beg to defer. Because, if I just name the followings from the exact same era: '*War* by Edwin Starr' or '*Imagine* by John Lennon', almost immediately many would recognize those protest songs! Why? Because their writers had a different approach in their political or protest song writing, which made their songs timeless. All the named performers were popular in the same era, all became hit songs in their own rights but only a few like 'War' or 'Imagine' are still aired regularly, and stand out in that category even after so many decades.

In his musical contribution against war, Bob Dylan directly targets 'Eisenhower' and uses a more direct approach and harsh criticism through his song - 'Master of War'. In an interview with USA Today in Sep 10, 2001, Bob Dylan says: "*...It's speaking against what Eisenhower was calling a military industrial complex as he was making his exit from the presidency. That spirit was in the air, and I picked it up.*"

On the contrary, John Lennon takes a 'soft' and an indirect approach in his song 'Imagine'. His target audience is not a particular individual or those in the administration. He is talking to you, to me and to the people all over the world, and he does not show any sign of frustration in his delivery.

John Lennon softly 'suggests', delicately 'raises awareness', and gently 'invites' people to think about the policy, about the way things are run, and to envision peace.

Clearly today, the history shows that perhaps a 'soft' and 'objective' approach in writing protest songs can be more influential and powerful, even for generations to come.

In another example, similar to Richie Havens' Handsome Johnny, Erwin Starr's song War, also asks some questions about war. But Norman Whitfield and Barrett Strong (the songwriters for 'War') they question not only the very existence of war but strategically place their question right at the beginning of their song, immediately followed by a catchy answer.

Contrary to 'Handsome Johnny', 'War' names no borders or specific country, hence the lyrics stay global and relatable to all.

Whitfield first produced that anti-Vietnam War protest song with The Temptations (an American vocal group) as the original vocalists. When Motown Label began to receive considerable requests to release 'War' as a single, Whitfield re-recorded the song with Edwin Starr as its solo vocalist. Starr's version of 'War' was a number-one hit on the Billboard Hit 100 chart in 1970, and not only it is considered as the most successful and well-known song of Erwin's career, but also one of the most popular protest songs ever recorded.

However the lyrics of 'War' reminds the destruction of innocent lives and shattering dreams, it does not give the "warning siren" for yet another bomb or missiles coming - as we can hear in the lyrics for 'Handsome Johnny'.

The song 'War' touches human feelings and speaks to mankind heart–to–heart, especially when it refers to 'tears of mothers' eyes and loss of their sons' lives'.

In conclusion, *as a songwriter, your expressed view in your song defines the 'type', 'depth', 'extent' and 'length' of the relationship amongst the vocal artists, their audience and the message itself. Your expression and choice of words govern the distance amongst all three, both in terms of **'time'** and **'space'.** A well-chosen point of view can transcend time to make a message song contemporary at all times.*

Now let us next, outline types of message songs.

Among types of message songs I can name (but not limited to):

Social Songs – addressing issues such as:

- ✓ Equality
- ✓ Justice & Fairness
- ✓ Liberty
- ✓ Freedom (expression/movement)
- ✓ Peace & Security
- ✓ Community / Unity
- ✓ Change
- ✓ Crime
- ✓ Public Education & Literacy

Humanity Songs – addressing issues such as:

- ✓ Rights & Responsibilities
- ✓ Health & Well-being
- ✓ Morality
- ✓ Empathy & Sympathy / Mentality
- ✓ Hope, Drive & Motivation
- ✓ Dialogue, Understanding & Cross-cultures

Call for Action Songs – addressing issues such as:

- ✓ Environment / Global Warming
- ✓ Sustainability
- ✓ Poverty

Commemorative / Celebratory Songs – recalling, reminding or emphasizing topics/events of significance in history and in life of human being such as:

- ✓ Remembrance Day
- ✓ International Day of Friendship
- ✓ International Day of Happiness
- ✓ World Teacher's Day - etc.

Here one may ask, *'Isn't writing social or humanity message songs kind of political?'* Well, it depends what your objective is, what angle you are targeting to cover, and what type of words you are using to tackle a particular issue. It also depends on your point of view, tune and the way you express your words both musically and visually, and that how objective you stay with your core message as a social or humanity song.

There is never a single aspect to a social or humanity issue. A message song won't be a political one, unless you intentionally want it to be.

SAMPLES OF MESSAGE SONG

Here are a few samples of my message songs in various topics for you to study *(They are available for streaming from Spotify or from artist or author's music sites)*:

Sample 1*: A social – humanity message song

Topic: Social Equality / Morality / Sympathy & Empathy
Vocalist: Kate Todd
Songwriters: Mosi Dorbayani & Saadi
Orchestration Amarita; **Producer:** Peter Linseman

I'm just a human with morality

A being with feelings and vitality

I am my words, I am my verse

Perhaps a familiar voice with few concerns

I'm no Politician or an Activist

I'm no Hero or a Factivist

I've just a few words to say
They aren't bitter or meant to cause dismay
Human beings are members of a whole
In creation of one essence and soul
If one member is afflicted with pain
Other members uneasy will remain
If we have no sympathy for human pain
The name of human we cannot retain
If we have no sympathy, it's inhumane
In the name of love, we need to make a change
So, let's put ourselves in perspective
This is a should and not a may be
Let's not step on each other's hopes and dreams
Make us suffer and crumple our beliefs
Human beings are members of a whole
In creation of one essence and soul
If one member is afflicted with pain
Other members uneasy will remain.

Translation of Saadi's verse by: Arianpour

*For more details about this song and its background story, go to 'Notes for Further Thought' – an interview with the author, on page 88

Sample 2*: A social ethics message song

Topic: Social Ethics & Behavior
Vocalist: Kyle Shedrick
Songwriter: Mosi Dorbayani
Orchestration / Arrangement: Andysh

In the city of ambitions drive carefully

Know the conditions and move mindfully

At Yellow check your emotions...

understand sensations, the rushes for progressions

When saw the first green, give the signal to the Right

Turn to your Heart and always stay clear

Never pass a red light...

don't worry...

you won't stay behind

Keep going on the Integrity Avenue

Avoid Losers' lane, speed up just with positive attitude

In the city of Ambitions drive carefully

Know the conditions and move mindfully

At Dignity and Temptation stop, check both ends

Mind where your turning ends

When take the Right turn, in no time you'll see...

your destination is at the corner of Happiness and Success

Keep going on the Integrity Avenue

Avoid Losers' lane to bypass,...

speed up just with positive attitude

Once took the Right turn, in no time you'll see...

your destination is at the corner of Happiness and Success

In the city of Ambitions drive carefully

Know the conditions and move mindfully,

Move mindfully,

Move mindfully.

* For more details about this song and its background story, go to 'Notes for Further Thought' – an interview with the author, on page 89

Sample 3*: A celebratory message song

Topic: Friendship / International Day of Friendship
Vocalist: Krista Earle
Songwriter: Mosi Dorbayani
Orchestration / Arrangement: Andysh

Oh, you...

you are hard to find...

harder to leave...

impossible to forget

Oh, you...

you are so selfless...

you uplift the soul and....

comfort me, when in trouble

When love left me in tears...

you, put smile on my face...

and never judged me for my mistakes

you never judged me for my mistakes

Oh, you...

you are a tear drop in the ocean...

a rare one to find...

but still the best to confide

Oh, you...

you are so selfless, ...

you uplift the soul and...

comfort me, when in trouble

When promises were not kept,...

dreams turned into nightmares,...

you gave me courage to move on

Oh, you gave me courage to move on

*For more details about this song and its background story, go to 'Notes for Further Thought' – an interview with the author, on page 90

Sample 4*: A commemorative message song

Topic: Nelson Mandela / International Day of Mandela
Vocalist: Nasambu
Songwriter: Mosi Dorbayani
Orchestration/Arrangement: The Mystic Nomads

Oh, Madiba...

you conquered the fear

taught love to peers...

and gave us freedom we long desired

Oh, Madiba...

you mastered the fate

lead our souls to a grace...

...and gave us hopes for brighter day

Oh, you my Madiba...

you gave us courage to make...

the impossible possible

taught us to stay positive and responsible

Oh, Madiba...

every time I fall...

I know I will rise again

for I will regain my strengths once again

Oh, my Madiba...

I will never forget...

your impact on my life

and on what I call it my Human Rights

Oh, Madiba

you conquered the fear

taught love to peers...

and gave us freedom we long desired

*For more details about this song and its background story, go to 'Notes for Further Thought' – an interview with the author, on page 90 & 91

Sample 5*: A social message song

Topic: Unity / Community / Care / Think of Future
Vocalist: Mike DeCole
Songwriter: Mosi Dorbayani

The moment that you realize...

there's so much pain before your eyes

The time that you understand...

you've got the pen or mic in your hand

You no longer can sit and stare

just pray problems vanish in thin air

For how long we should drift alone...

isn't it all that we have ever known?

We keep driving through the night...

but is it sure we are heading for the light?

For how long should moments pass...

let regrets forever last?

When are we gonna save...

the flickering lights that begin to fade?

*For more details about this song and its background story, go to 'Notes for Further Thought' – an interview with the author, on page 92

Sample 6*: A humanity message song

Topic: Hope / Drive & Motivation
Vocalist: Anthony Tullo
Lyricist: Mosi Dorbayani
Composer: David Lipari Jr; **Producer:** Peter Linseman

Vision without action is only daydreaming

Action without vision is just a nightmare

Won't take much to dream

And if you don't go for it...

what's your life gonna be about?

You are one, but you are!

You can't do everything, but can do something

Have faith, have hope

Don't you dare to give up on your dreams

Have dreams, your dreams...

Have dreams, dare to dream

Don't let what you can't, interfere with what you can do

Build a castle in your dreams...

then its foundation in reality

Work harder, push farther till it's caught in reality

Live your dreams, don't care what people say

Dream big, think bigger, work harder...

till you make it real

Tell yourself now...

what it takes gonna hurt sometime

and maybe less pleasing that you wanna

Have courage, you gonna get what you always wanna

See it through and measure every step

Dream big, think bigger, work harder...

till you make it real

Have dreams, your dreams

Have dreams, dare to dream

Dare to dream.

*For more details about this song and its background story, go to 'Notes for Further Thought' – an interview with the author, on page 93

Sample 7*: A humanity message song

Topic: Hope / Drive & Motivation
Vocalist: Mike DeCole
Songwriter: Mosi Dorbayani

Remember, not unless you make 'Progress' for your goal

the theater of life won't cast you for major roles

Behind you are full of challenges...

but before you are still new opportunities

The key to attainment, fame and success...

is to push your limits harder nonetheless

Never stop doing your best...

feeling out there no one cares

When life gives you reasons to cry...

show life you have more reasons to smile

Just like every night that turns into day

tough times shall pass and fade away

When life gives you reasons to cry...

show life you have more reasons to smile.

The key to attainment, fame and success...

is to push your limits harder nonetheless.

*For more details about this song and its background story, go to 'Notes for Further Thought' – an interview with the author, on page 93

Sample 8*: A social message song

Topic: Care / Social Care / Change / Change of mentality
Vocal & Melody: Tehillah Henry
Lyricist: Mosi Dorbayani
Composer / Arranger: Amarita

It's a sadness that can't be spoken

A kind of pain that goes on and on

It's like a clock ticking,...

ticking for a tomorrow that never comes

It feels like an ocean

The waves that come and go

A constant rhythm,...

a rhythm that forever flows

Are we ever going to learn...

how to end this tragedy?

Let the sight of shore go ...

to cross the ocean and meet reality

How can we just sit and stare?

Pretend problems aren't for us to care

How can we just ignore facts?

Pray problems to vanish with no act

Are we ever going to realize...

there is so much pain before our eyes?

Are we ever going to understand...

we have the power for change in our hands?

*For more details about this song and its background story, go to 'Notes for Further Thought' – an interview with the author, on page 94

Sample 9*: A humanity / social message song

Topic: Voicing Your Concern / Dialogue / Resuming Relations
Vocalists: Jess Braun
Songwriter: Mosi Dorbayani
Orchestration / Arrangement: Amarita

It's time to break our silence

Roar it out like mighty lions

It's time to speak our mind

Say what bothers us and unwind

It's time to end our sadness

Hang up calls for any madness

It's time for us to leave behind...

Everything we can't refine

All we need is willingness...

To listen and go for happiness

We shouldn't let anything make us dull

Or our past choices force us to fall

We shouldn't let our moments pass

Let regret, forever last

It's time to break our silence

Roar it out like mighty lions

It's time to speak our mind

Say what bothers us and unwind.

*For more details about this song and its background story, go to 'Notes for Further Thought' – an interview with the author, on page 94 & 95

PLAY & SING ALONG: PIANO SCORE FOR MESSAGE SONG - 'IT'S TIME' (Lyrics P 62-63)

It's Time!

Songwriter: Mosi Dorbayani, SOCAN/ASCAP - Jan 2017

11
roar it out like migh - ty lions it's time to speak our mind
hang up calls for a - ny mad - ness it's time for us to li -
14
1.
say what bo - thers us and un - wind 2.It's
ve be - hind e - ve - ry - thing we
1.
17
2.
can't re - fine...
2.
20
All we need is will

23
- ing - ness.. to lis-ten and go for hap - pi - ness
26
All we need is will - ing- ness... to lis-ten and go for hap
29
- pi - ness We shouldn't let a-ny- thing make us dull
32
or our past choi-ces force us to fall We shouldn't let our mo

35
- ments pass
let reg - ret
fo -
37
re- ver last
It's
time to end our sad -
39
ness
hang up calls
for a - ny mad - ness it's
42
time for us to li - ve be - hind
e - ve - ry- thing we

45
can't re-fine
We shouldn't let a-ny thing make us dull
48
or our past choi-ces force us to fall
We shouldn't let our mo
51
-ments pass
let reg - ret fo -
53
re- ver last
It's
time to break our si -
time to end our sad -

A PDF format of this music sheet / score can be obtained from WAALM Publications.

A PIECE OF RECORDED HISTORY

Message songs are often pieces of recorded history. While many of them beautifully serve their purposes

for raising bars for social awareness and social activism, some of them remain truly everlasting and engraved in the book of history. Often such songs get the chance to be academically studied as part of social sciences, popular culture, and research for humanity or arts.

Social movements, social activism, and progressive thoughts influence popular culture, and most certainly popular culture – music in particular is one of the best and most effective medium for recording and encapsulating such endeavours.

Popular culture, especially popular songs are among the most effective tools for self-expression, communication, raising concerns or even healing social wounds.

Through exploration of lyrics, music becomes a tool that offers social studies an opportunity to engage in meaningful conversations about major social issues. Perhaps it is part of every responsible historian, social science educator and songwriter with interest in writing message songs to analyze the historical role that music has played in raising social consciousness.

In that respect, here I would like to share with you a few examples as case studies, and begin this by writing about one of my favourite songs, which in my opinion is a brilliant example for studying the role of message songs in recording a piece of history.

It is 1969, the racism, injustice and inequality for black people in the United States is still a hot topic. However many songs are written and performed to highlight such social inequality, one song tops them all. Anguish, anger, confession, strive, hope, protest, and poetry ALL can be heard in a beautiful soulful song titled: *'Is it because I'm Black?' By Syl Johnson*

Syl Johnson's social message song — if it is not what got many out to march against their fear to demand for their basic human rights — it is certainly what made many black people to deeply think and to seriously re-evaluate their circumstances. *It is by far one of the most socially conscious pieces of songwriting of its time.*

It not only portrays the appalling situation of colored people in the 60s and early 70s, but also makes a serious statement of black pride with a sad blues groove.

This seven-and-a-half-minute track represents the voice of a generation who is trying their hardest to overcome oppression and yet to survive and carry on their generation to the next to ensure that their legacy lives on in a new and hopefully better society. A society where segregation and racism is not tolerated.

In his song, 'Is it because I'm black?' Syl Johnson asks a question, which so many people could ask of their own circumstances. Brown, red, yellow all could ask the same question from themselves and relate to it.

*In 2010 Craig Charles of BBC Radio 6, asks Syl Johnson about the background to that song and Syl replies:

"...It was when Dr. Luther King was killed. I never intended to make a radical song [some people took it that way]. It's a song that is just asking a question: Is it because I'm black, these things happen? ...It wasn't playing for the whites then, but now all young whites are taking it out. ...Those who want to hear that message now, are young white people."

Sadly, it seems Syl Johnson's question is still pretty much valid and relevant to many in the 21st century. Be it the case of white supremacy or immigration, gender inequality, or foreign policy and trade—the recent events in the US proves that there is still a mountain to climb and unfortunately that is not limited to the United States.

Personally, I'm not black nor an American, but as a white proud Canadian, hereby I would like to thank each and every black individual who peacefully made sacrifices to end segregation around the world; and I would like to extend my appreciation and gratitude to people of all colors, who strive for peace and living in harmony.

Moving on, musically speaking, 'Is it because I'm black?' has awesome bass line and drum groove. The song enters the vein and penetrates the soul. The song hit No. 11 on the Billboard R&B chart in 1969, giving us some insights into the pulse of the times.

* *https://numerogroup.wordpress.com/tag/craig-charles*

SOCIAL MOVEMENTS AND SOLIDARITY

Social movements can rearrange traditions. Culture changes. A large group of people can transform their values and adopt new patterns of behavior, or simply set a new and different terms for it.

And here, music is a key component of social movements. Music is a major part of culture and serves as an important mechanism for solidarity.

The Concert for Bangladesh - Album Cover

A case study: The very first such social movements and solidarity, which was facilitated by music stage, got conducted by Georg Harrison (1943–2001), the former member of Beatles in 1971.

The event was in response to a request from Ravi Shankar (1920–2012), a Bengali Indian musician and a composer of Hindustani classical music, and the mission was to raise money to aid starving refugees during the 'Bangladesh Liberation War'.

The show welcomed 40,000 spectators and opened with a performance by Shankar followed by many stellar artists such as Bob Dylan, Georg Harrison, Eric Clapton, Billy Preston, Ringo Starr, Leon Russell and

Madison Square Garden, NY - The Concert for Bangladesh 1971
Image Source: clickittefaq.com

many more, who mounted the stage to lend their talents to the cause.

For the first time in the history of musical stage, the dynamic between political statements and popular music changed, when Madison Square Garden accommodated the first ever large concert to benefit a humanitarian cause.

The musicians donated their time and talents which was supplemented by a live-performance recorded triple album and a feature-length concert film.

The live concert and its supplementary productions not only raised millions of dollars to aid suffering people of East Pakistan (today Bangladesh) in severe weather, but also raised global awareness of the situation in that region to end war and genocidal rape.

George Harrison's initiative and the Concert for Bangladesh set the example and led the way for many benefit events or concerts for humanity throughout the following decades.

UNICEF honoured George Harrison and Ravi Shankar with the 'Child Is the Father of Man' award at an annual ceremony in recognition of their fundraising efforts for Bangladesh.

Following the footsteps of Harrison and Shankar, still today we can see responsible artists around the world, who contribute to humanitarian causes close to their hearts.

PEACE AND HARMONY

The Woodstock Music Festival, 1969, New York

A case study: *The Woodstock Music and Art Fair (the Woodstock Festival) was advertised as a three-day peace and music event (Aug. 15-18, 1969) and featured 32 of the most iconic artists in American music history.

However marked as the greatest hippie event of all time, Woodstock was more than just a festival, it captured the free spirit of the 1960s perfectly and became a cultural-artistic landmark that represents an entire generation of American youth.

This for-profit event was held on a 600-acre dairy farm outside of tiny Bethel, New York. It was organized and promoted by Michael Lang, John P. Roberts, Joel Rosenman, and Artie Kornfeld.

Richie Havens played the opening act, and the bill for the next three days included, among others: Santana, Joan Baez, Jefferson Airplane, Janis Joplin, Crosby, Stills, Nash & Young, Joe Cocker, Creedence Clearwater Revival, and The Band. Jimi Hendrix closed the festival on Monday morning.

*Around 186,000 advance tickets were sold, and the organizers anticipated approximately 200,000 people would turn up, but surprisingly over 400,000 showed up to hear the big names play on stage in the field.

The Woodstock Ceremony Aug. 15. 1969

The place was not equipped to provide sanitation or first aid for that many unexpected number of people attending. Hundreds of thousands found themselves in a struggle against bad weather, food shortages, and poor sanitation.

Roads were jammed for miles. The huge crowd of people began to overwhelm the small rural community. New York governor Nelson Rockefeller considered sending the National Guard, but the organizers convinced him not to, while Sullivan County actually declared a state of emergency.

Aerial Photo - The Woodstock Festival 1969

Reportedly, due to road traffic jams, medicine, drinking water and food had to be flown in by helicopters.

To prevent food and water price increase, both the organizers and local sheriff joined their efforts for free food and water distribution.

Despite of its massive crowd and logistical problem, the event was absolutely peaceful. There were only two recorded fatalities: one from a heroin overdose, and another caused in an accident when a tractor ran over an attendee sleeping in a nearby hayfield.

There were also two recorded giving births at the event. One in a car caught in traffic jam and the other in a hospital after an airlift by helicopter. The festival's chief medical officer, Dr. William Abruzzi told Rolling Stone magazine: *"These people are really beautiful. There has been no violence whatsoever which is really remarkable for a crowd of this size."*

*The backers of the festival lost about $2 million, and faced about 80 lawsuits, which were filed against Woodstock Ventures, primarily by farmers in the area. But the organizers called it a success because of its peaceful atmosphere. The producers could make money from the movie and the soundtrack of the festival, which helped them to eventually pay off their debts.

**About the financial shortfall, the producer Michael Lang said to American Heritage: *"Today is a time to think about what happened here - the youth culture came out of the alleys and the streets. This generation was brought together and showed it was beautiful."*

WHAT WOODSTOCK FESTIVAL TEACHES US?

After the assassination of John F. Kennedy, Dr. Martin Luther King, Malcolm X and Robert F. Kennedy, people really needed such a festival.

The Vietnam War was scorching television and radio speakers and people needed an event to come together in harmony to express peace.

In tune with the idealistic hopes and dreams of the 1960s, perhaps Woodstock festival was an awesome experience for most people who were there.

Showing the sign of Victory for Peace - Woodstock Music Festival

It evidently brought people closer to each other and gave them a sense of social harmony, which along with the quality of music, and the overwhelming mass of people with their hippie clothing, behavior, and attitude, helped to make it one of the most enduring events of the 20th century.

* http://worldofwonder.net ** www.americanheritage.com

After the festival, Max Yasgur, who owned the site where Woodstock was held, said: *"I saw it as a victory for peace, love and understanding."*

With no doubt, Woodstock was the most influential musical event that spread the message of peace towards the close of the decade in 1969.

Perhaps what we can learn from Woodstock festival is how half a million people who faced the potential for all sorts of disturbance, violence, and disaster, instead, chose to spend three days with music, all in peace and harmony.

The Peaceful Attendees at Woodstock Festival

The historic event of Woodstock registers and proves us that music has the ultimate power to unite masses in peace and harmony, like no other form of art ever can.

NOTES FOR FURTHER THOUGHT

AN INTERVIEW WITH THE AUTHOR

The following is an extract from the original interview conducted by Diplomatic Journal – Arts for Diplomacy Podcast, Wales - UK:

DJ: Why song writing?

MD: *Because words matter. And once they are delivered melodically, they find a better chance to engage human's emotion.*

DJ: Why is it important to engage people through arts, music or songs in particular?

MD: *Things like how to hunt or fish, how to build shelter, road, dam, canal, or even flying to the Moon and back have never been a major challenge for human being. The biggest challenge for human being was and still is human being! To understand and being understood. To love and being loved.*

In order to have that essential engagement to meet such challenges, we need a medium, a tool if you will – to enable us to get closer to one another. And perhaps songs are the best medium to establish such interactions. Thanks to the power of songs, people open up, let go of things, show love, respect, contribute and engage. Many fall in love and make love because of songs they hear.

DJ: How did it all happen for you?

MD: *When I was in high school, I got inspired by some of Shakespeare's plays, as well as Rumi and Saadi's poetries and like most teenagers of my era, I fell in love with the rich sounds of the popular music of the 70s.*

I started to write some poems and wrote almost 40 pages in my notebook during my high school senior years. One day in hope for some guidance and perhaps a few words of encouragement or validation, I dared to show my notebook to my literature instructor.

"If I may, I wrote some poems and I was wondering if you could kindly have a look at them and furnish me with your valuable thoughts", I asked.

With a cold face, he took my notebook reluctantly, scrolled quickly and without even reading a word of it, he threw it back at me and said: "Not unless you have read 3000 pages of poetry and memorized 300 to 400 of them, you should jot down anything."

Well, that was it, sadly he killed it for me in front of everyone. I stopped writing poems until 2004, when I saw the movie 'De-Lovely', a musical production based on life story of songwriter 'Cole Porter' played by Kevin Kline.

That movie touched me and sparked writing musical literature in me. I kept writing every now and then but with no intension of making them public. A quiet passion, if you will.

In 2005 along with my wife, Marjan, we co-founded WAALM Awards in England and Wales, which soon became one of the top 10 awarding bodies in the world and as the result, I rubbed shoulders with many artists, writers, poets, singers, songwriters, actors and producers around the world and my exposure to world's culture got deeper day by day – even after WAALM branched out to Canada.

It was in 2011 when WAALM introduced 'Leonardo Tajabadi' a Baritone opera singer, based in Paris to me and informed me that he wants to have a conversation with me about a new progressive style in opera.

He said that during his tour in Florence, he was introduced to 'Rock Opera' and he spoke passionately about it. He asked if I would be interested to support. I kept that in my mind while WAALM was collaborating with him on other musical projects.

A couple of months later, one night during my visit to Budapest in late summer, I decided to walk along the Danube. I was listening to a classical radio when 'Moonlight Sonata' by Beethoven came on. Coincidently, I could see the reflection of the moon on the river too and suddenly the words were striking my head. There and then on my Dictaphone I recorded and wrote 'Moonlight Shimmer' on Beethoven's sonata and next day had it arranged in Rock style by Lai from Vietnam for Leonard to record.

Leonardo recorded the first version of 'Moonlight Shimmer' in Rock-Opera in Paris and WAALM officially published it. It became popular and got broadcast by Radios and TVs in Europe and covered by other singers in various styles in other continents as well – including a beautiful rendition by Soprano Carolina Ghigliazza from Argentina, accompanied by a masterful piano by Maestra Marta Bellido.

'Moonlight Shimmer' became my first official release in 2011, one of the only two Beethoven pieces ever recorded with words.

The interesting part of the story is that later, I learned Beethoven composed his sonata in summer of 1801 on an estate belonging to the Count Anton II Brunswick family near Budapest. It is absolutely amazing how the music and the words got composed 211 years apart but in the same season and in the same country!

I still feel honored to be the first, who wrote words on Beethoven's Moonlight Sonata. And I am happy that it is translated into other languages and performed by many notable sopranos and tenors around the world.

DJ: While you have a considerable number of successful romantic or 'love' songs, you equally emphasize on intellectual and serious 'message songs' with social themes. Why you diversified your repertoire in that way?

MD: *To me, 'romance' and 'love of humanity' are both valuable and important; therefore, I give both of them the care and attention they deserve. There are thousands of songwriters out there who write about love in different context, but there is only a thin layer who can, or are willing to address issues facing humanity through music.*

DJ: Majority of your songs are categorized as 'intellectual' songs on digital outlets and reviews on social sites indicate that people found them meaningful. Even the stories in some of your songs were painted on canvas by some drawing artists. How your songs reached to this quality?

MD: *I try to avoid creating something that is unnecessary. Be it a love song or a message song, I write when I genuinely have something new to say and more importantly from an angle that to best of my knowledge either only a few or nobody ever said it before.*

For example, my love songs such as: 'Blue Jay & Red Cardinal'; 'When I'm with You'; 'Hey Artist'; 'Reason for Soiree'; 'You Made Me Whole Again'; 'Lost in Thoughts of You'; 'Yours Truly'; 'All the Way with You' or 'Love Is on Its Way' – they are all composed in a way that they can paint a picture of a mature love story for listeners to imagine and relate to; and of course, in doing so, words have to be descriptive and colorful.

Even my songs about separation or failure of love such as 'My Last Teardrop' still paints that picture for the listener, but of course in darker colors.

You cannot paint a picture with your song if the lyrics is just a couple of phrases with fifteen times repeating baby, baby, oh baby, baby or a catchy phrase or word which is repeated for eighteen times in three and half minutes.

I also believe formal education, age and life experience are influential too. When a songwriter is still young, perhaps they see love and world differently, but as they grow older and become more mature, their outlook changes and their songs perhaps become deeper in meaning.

DJ: We would like to ask you about some of your specific message songs. Recently you wrote message songs titled 'To whom It May Concern' and 'In the City of Ambitions'. Tell us more about these two projects.

MD: *'To Whom It May Concern' is a social message song for humanity. I wrote it to highlight the world day of social equality and justice on 20th February. In that song I barrowed a few words from the Persian poet of the medieval period, Saadi (1210–1291), which is written on top of the entrance of the United Nations hall in New York.*

'To Whom It May Concern' talks about social and human morality and invites people to respect each other's rights and it asks people, including

governments not to afflict pain on humanity. It emphasizes on living in harmony.

It is voiced by talented Canadian Musician/Singer-songwriter/Actor, Kate Todd, and produced by Peter Linseman, a dedicated professional, who is leading Music Mentor Productions in Toronto. Their contributions to this project are truly admirable. Kate is one of my favourite artists of all time and I love her vocal qualities.

The song 'In the City of Ambitions' is recorded by the American singer, Kyle Shedrick, who is based in New York. It is a Metaphoric song for Social Ethics & Behavior.

There is a fine but blurry line between 'Ambition and Greed'. Sadly, in today's fast-paced world, some have real hard time to realize the difference.

Greed makes us self-centered. It may rise us up in the society at the expense of others and often that seems natural to us simply because the ultimate objective is about ourselves. Greed is an illusion that tells us we should have it all because we deserve it.

Ambition however, is about having the desire to create change. Its best version is about working for a cause selflessly. Ambition is often inclusive, i.e. inviting others to join and share your ride. BUT in the 'City of Ambitions', where people CANNOT realize or distinguish the difference between the two, you'd better drive carefully ☺.

In this song, the social ethics and behavior are metaphorically depicted as driving through the city and dos and don'ts for attainment and success are suggested in form of a navigation, codes of conduct and traffic lights.

Kyle did this project masterfully and his vocal harmonies made it so especial. This project was orchestrated and arranged by Andysh, a creative composer from Armenia.

DJ: You wrote a celebratory song for the international day of friendship. Any insight on that?

MD: *Yes, I wrote 'Oh You My Friend' to celebrate 30th July, the international day of friendship. That project is recorded by a sensational Canadian vocalist, Krista Earle, who later adopted Krissi Hunter as for her artistic name. She connected with that project well and conveyed the essence of the words very well.*

The instrumentals for that project were all recorded live in studio, supervised and engineered by Andysh.

In my view, a good friend contributes to the fullness of life, but finding an authentic, honest, and trust worthy one is rare.

Personally, I do not have many friends, but I understand the importance of having a good one.

Genuine friends can assist us to realize, define and live a meaningful life.

DJ: In honor of Nelson Mandela, you wrote a song titled: 'Madiba'. Please tell us more about this title.

MD: *The United Nations named 18th July as the international day of Nelson Mandela. To mark his contribution for humanity and human rights, I wrote the song, 'Madiba'.*

The word 'Madiba' has roots in the 18th century Africa. Nelson Mandela is often addressed as 'Tata Madiba' meaning father of Xhosa clan. The name 'Madiba' represents his ancestry and is used as a sign of respect and affection.

**According to Richard Pithouse, a politics professor at Rhodes University in South Africa 'Madiba' would be used in "an intimate context"; therefore, I used it for my song honoring and celebrating his life.*

Undoubtedly, Nelson Mandela was one of the major champions of peace and human rights, whose significant contribution for social justice made him an icon.

When I decided to write a song in his honor, I wanted it to be in two versions. One in Pop-afro and the other in Afro-blues with traditional African vibe.

The Pop version is voiced by Elisabeth Popp, a singer from Copenhagen, Denmark and the Afro-blues version is recorded by Nasambu from Kenya with a musical arrangement by The Mystic Nomads.

Nasambu's rendition in Afro-blues captured the hearts of many, and her version got played at the United Nations, during Youth for Human Rights international summit in 2014.

* usatoday.com – Dec. 06. 2013

DJ: Your message song, 'Flickering Lights', which was nominated for the best R&B at the 8th annual Hollywood Music in Media Awards of 2017, in Los Angeles - California, poke those, like yourself who are equipped with microphone and pen, to address social issues. Who is the subject matter in this song?

MD: *'Flickering Lights' invites people to put aside their self-serving individualism and indifference for the sake of our youths' future; it emphasizes on unity for a sustainable community growth.*

Everybody who has a voice, and the ability to write and create should lend their voice and talent to their communities to raise social awareness. Everyone who has the power of mic and pen and the ability to articulate, must address issues facing our future generations. And I'm not talking just locally, but globally too.

'Flickering Lights' are our Youths and their future, who are being ignored in many ways in many societies.

I am absolutely thrilled that this song is well-received and got nominated. I dubbed Mike De'cole, who voiced that project as the 'Knight of R&B'.

His skillful smoky voice speaks for itself. He works on his projects like a craftsman and is a dedicated professional. Personally, I love his voice and his songs are in my music player 24/7. Chicago presented the world with several finest vocal artists of all time, and I think Mike's name soon will be recognized equally to those before him, whose musical influence reached all over the world.

DJ: Tell us about your project 'Dare to Dream'.

MD: *Well, perhaps one of the elements that keeps human being alive is 'hope'. This song asks people to hold on to that and stay positive. It is to motivate and encourage people to strive for their goals and dreams relentlessly.*

Perhaps similar to 'High Hopes', which was written and performed by Tim Scott McConnell, and covered by Bruce Springsteen, in 'Dare to Dream' I broke all the rules of lyrics writing. Its music is composed by David Lipari Jr. who is based in the US and it is recorded by Anthony Tullo, a Canadian rising Country-rock star with vigorous voice.

Anthony recorded it at Music Mentor Productions and Peter Linseman did its sound engineering and mastering. This project has a very cool video promo, which is produced by WAALM.

DJ: Is your other project, 'Limitless' in line with the same concept – motivation and hope?

MD: *Absolutely, but in a different context.*

Promoting and defending a shared spirit of human solidarity and support takes many forms — the simplest of which can be a friendly life coaching.

In 'Limitless' words are coaching listeners on how to attain success through hardworking and perseverance. This project is part of an EP album titled: 'May, and Everything After', by Mike De'cole.

DJ: Recently you wrote a message song named 'Ocean without Shore'. What is this track about?

MD: *It says ignorance is NOT a bliss and humanity should step out of their comfort zone to face the realities of life. The sooner we face the challenges the better. By turning a blind eye, or just praying, the problems won't go away.*

Its composition and arrangement in Pop-classical is done by Amarita, a classically trained composer based in Romania and is voiced by very talented musician and singer, Tehillah Henry (Tilly), from Wolverhampton, England, who is one of the most played artists on BBC Radio and BBC WM 95.6 FM.

DJ: Your latest message song in 2017 is called 'It's Time'. It can be interpreted in various forms. Please give us some insight on this song.

MD: *Yes, it can be interpreted differently. While it is encouraging couples, partners, or friends to talk it through, to communicate and resume their relations, it can also be interpreted as words of encouragement for people and communities to voice their concern, speak up about their issues and engage through dialogue.*

I see people from different walks of life who are unhappy with their certain circumstances or their relationships, but still reluctant to talk about it or are shy to establish dialogue with their partner or their communities.

'It's Time' emphasizes on having dialogue, reaching to an agreement and moving forward.

This project is voiced by Jess Braun, a vocal powerhouse talent based in Austin, but originally from Richmond, Virginia.

She was discovered by WAALM Productions and introduced to me to collaborate. I'm happy to have her amongst the vocal artists in my roster.

DJ: Any particular signer or band, which you believe world should hear more about them and get to know their talents?

MD: *'Gwawr Edwards' (Soprano from Wales); 'Alessandro Safina' (Tenor from Siena, Italy); 'Alessandra Paonessa' (Soprano from Toronto, Canada); 'Arlene Paculan' (Singer-songwriter from Mississauga, Canada); and 'Anne Geraghty' (Soprano from Ottawa, Canada) to name a few.*

DJ: Among international superstars, who are your favourites?

MD: *Maestro 'Andrea Bocelli' (Italian Pop-tenor) and Maestro 'Sattar' (Persian-American Pop-tenor). I also enjoy listening to 'Barbra Streisand' (American Singer/Actress); 'Jamiroquai' (British Funk and Acid jazz band); 'A-ha' (Norwegian Pop-rock band) 'Chris Rea' (English Singer-songwriter and guitarist) and of course the legend, 'Frank Sinatra'.*

DJ: Did you have academic studies for songwriting?

MD: *Yes, I benefited from a short course in Songwriting, instructed by Prof. Pat Pattison from Berklee College of Music. I found his teaching methodology practical and motivational.*

I highly recommend attending his seminars and courses to all enthusiasts, even those with songwriting experience.

DJ: You donate all your songs to WAALM, a registered non-profit organization for arts, music and literature. Why is that?

MD: *As a founding member of WAALM, I know that they can use my productions and songs to facilitate the promotion of 'Cross-cultures' and 'Cultural Diplomacy'. All proceeding incomes, if any, goes to supporting independent artists, art productions, cultural education, and promotion of those true talents who deserve to be discovered and recognized.*

Through WAALM's facilitation, artists, writers and producers find opportunities to work with each other, share their resources and talents, give credit and recognition to each other and expand their network beyond their borders...

QUESTIONS FOR CONTEMPLATION / DISCUSSION

1. *How do you use 'words' in your daily life?*
2. *Are your words 'effective' in gaining what you want?*
3. *Do you think your words can 'shape' your character? How about shaping others'?*
4. *Have you ever 'influenced' someone with your words?*
5. *Often when people are happy, they 'hear' the beats of a song, but when sad, they 'listen' to its lyrics. Do you agree?*
6. *It is said while for Europeans 'lyrics' of a song is more important, for North Americans beats or the music of a song is of more interest. Do you have any preference in a song?*
7. *How often do you refer to a song / lyrics in your conversation with others?*
8. *Have you ever discussed or explored the message of a song with others?*
9. *What makes a song 'meaningful' to you?*
10. *If you were to write a message song, what your 'message' would be?*

ILLUSTRATED SONG

Impression of the artist from listening to the message song - **'To Whom It May Concern'**. [Lyrics p 46-47]

Drawing to the song: 'To Whom It May Concern' – by: Rumi Das

Mosi Dorbayani, the Author – Vancouver, Autumn 2017

ABOUT AUTHOR

Writing songs is another dimension of Mosi's life. As an entrepreneur, executive coach & consultant, adjunct professor in leadership & management, author, UDHR ambassador and humanitarian, he uses the topics and themes around him, applies his emotions, experiences from life and work, as well as the general feelings he has at the moment to write musical literature and melody.

"*Equally in this aspect of my life, I have been blessed and lucky to work with many true talents and vocal artists around the world who voice my songs and I am thankful to all of them*." Mosi says.

As a renowned cultural figure, author and international award winning writer, Mosi's words and songs are recorded and published by both signed and indie artists from over 25 countries, spanning 5 continents. Thus far, he has over 50 original recorded and published songs, including a few for The United Nations' international days, honoring and celebrating global commemorations.

As a librettist, he also contributed to a few short Operetta projects, including 'Consort me' and 'I am the one'. From Memphis to Paris, from Boston to Budapest, Mosi's songs are regularly played by most prominent radio stations around the world. Some of his visual songs are shown on Skyline and Transatlantic airlines and some including his recent classical *'Blue Jay & Red Cardinal'* is featured by VEVO, VOA TV and ATV.

Collaboration with Mosi has its own perks too, many artists in his roster got nominated and won awards from major music awarding bodies. Just recently, several of his songs and their recording artists got nominated for Hollywood Music in Media Awards in various genre.

Mosi holds a PhD in International Management and has published 11 books. He is represented by SOCAN / ASCAP and CMRRA.

WEBSITE:

www.dorbayani.com (click on menu: Lyrics/Songs)

CBC Radio Music Page:
http://artists.cbcmusic.ca/artist/52860

ReverbNation Page:
www.reverbnation.com/mosidorbayani

/MosiDorbayani

For collaboration & co-writing opportunities, forward your request to WAALM Productions at: waalm@gmx.us

Songs written by this author are available on **'Spotify'** and they can be downloaded from all the digital outlets including **'iTunes'**, **'Amazon MP3'** and **'CDBaby'**.

'MAY, AND EVERYTHING AFTER'

An EP album with 6 original tracks, all written by Mosi Dorbayani and voiced by the Knight of R&B, Mike De'cole.

'May, and everything after' not only sets the mood to dim the lights and play to have some romance, but also presents a blend of tune and words of incentives to elevate your spirit, when you need it most.

Available from all digital outlets and Spotify.

'VOICES OF ATTRACTION'

A full album, containing Mosi's recent hit songs, voiced by most talented international artists from around the world.

Visit the author's page for release & availability info.

ALSO FROM THIS AUTHOR:

- Business Samurai: Skills & Strategies for Leaders and Entrepreneurs – ISBN: 978-0-9940842-3-1
- Think About It – ISBN: 978-0-9940842-2-4
- Concise HR & Personnel – ISBN: 963 212 096 5
- Concise Economics – ISBN: 963 212 093 0
- Successful Business Organization – ISBN: 963 210 234 7
- Successful Management – ISBN: 963 210 233 9
- Successful Leadership – ISBN: 963 204 821 0
- Moderation Management Enlightened with Philosophy – ISBN: 963 210 699 7
- Hidden – ISBN 978-0-9940842-0-0
- Kojido Sogo Bujutsu: The Way of Persistence in Martial Arts – ISBN 978-0-9940842-1-7

www.ingramcontent.com/pod-product-compliance
Lightning Source LLC
LaVergne TN
LVHW052254100826
845147LV00001B/42

* 9 7 8 0 9 9 4 0 8 4 2 5 5 *